STOP THE MONKEY BUSINESS!

Eight WTFs That Can Make or Break You As A Leader and Manager

DAVID L. CLEVELAND

STOP THE MONKEY BUSINESS!

Eight WTFs That Can Make or Break You As A Leader and Manager

DAVID L. CLEVELAND

Goodyear, Arizona

Dedication

Oh, my goodness, there are so many people I could think of with regard to dedicating this book. It could be my mom. She pushed me with unwavering zeal to improve myself.

Maybe my wife Shirley, and my sons Kris and Josh, who I love dearly, for putting up with many years of international travel and my too often not being there when they needed me.

Perhaps it should be dedicated to Don Bowen, my Organizational Development Professor at University of Tulsa, who really opened my mind to the powers of organization and team, which helped me launch my first career in Human Resources.

Or later, as I started my career, Pete Cameron, the Gulf Oil Human Resources Executive who decided to give a 24-year-old, wet-behind-the-ears kid a chance to be Division Director of Personnel.

I also have to consider Georg Rosenbauer, the Hilti Executive who, after choosing me to run Human Resources at an early age, called me in and said, "…the other Division Presidents are tired of you telling them what to do and agree you should be put in charge of our smallest division in Latin America."

There are probably others. But I have to go with the guy who always believed in me, my dad. He always stood behind me, even when I probably didn't deserve it. He always told me, "Buddy, you can do anything you want if you put your mind to it."

Thanks Dad.

Contents

Endorsements

Stop the Monkey Business is an insightful and practical guide for managers and would-be managers in the world of business. The practical wisdom in this book is based on David's wide-ranging experience in leading a variety of businesses. While David's advice is well-grounded in substantive business concepts, he offers a pragmatic approach to applying those concepts in the workaday world of business. He emphasizes the need for a practical approach to leading an organization by demonstrating the necessity of an honest assessment of one's organization and the absolute necessity of good execution. His strong emphasis on making the customer the focus of everyone in the organization amounts to a "call-to-arms" for businesses that want to thrive in the face of fierce competition. His insistence that effective business leaders take a pragmatic approach to managing people, focus the company's resources where they are needed and solve problems on the fly, all in the name of serving customers is an essential lesson for business leaders today. Would-be managers, new managers, and long-serving managers can all benefit from reading this book.

-**Ralph W. Jackson,** Ph.D. Professor Emeritus
The Collins College of Business - University of Tulsa

This book is exceptional in its straight-talk style, clarity and execution, thus making it a powerful tool for all leaders and managers. The step-by-step strategies make it a fail-proof resource for everyone. The eight 'WTFs' are not only about how to 'Win The Future,' but also, 'What To Fix!'

-**Kristine A. Sexter,** Consultant and Author of *"Rolling Out the Recognition, Employee Retention Strategies for Manufacturers"*

I have worked with this sassy, down to earth and vocal leader for over 30 years. I even took his job when Hilti sent me to Tulsa Oklahoma while he got to become the President of the smallest Division. He achieved amazing results starting as a rookie GM of foreign territories in Latin America. All the time we worked together, Dave and I challenged each other and had great fun enjoying business and life with passion. He and his family are true friends who helped my family to become Americans.

This non-PhD unusual book reflects the true and honest way Dave acted as a motivational leader in whatever he did. Never a dull moment, never wasting time and always on the go challenging his teams at all levels to get results. In a very humorous way, it reflects simple and important learnings how to successfully conduct your life and do business. All recommendations are very practical and proven by facts of his career.

This book is an easy read, you will have fun and will smile when reflecting how his ideas and experiences compare to your conscious events in your own life.

-Andre Siegenthaler, retired Senior VP Human Resources with Hilti International and Hilti NA

Dave Cleveland writes in a funny, straightforward if irreverent, style that is easy to read and direct in its approach to the real-world issues facing managers today. He emphasizes sound principles with anecdotes from his extensive business career illustrating both successes and failings. It debunks some of the management theory I was taught in college some 50 years ago, which I realized after I moved into the real world and further reminded me that I'm not practicing some of the best management concepts even today. 'Stop The Monkey Business' WTF's are an eight-point guide to management success and, perhaps most importantly reminds us that we don't all have to fit a single mold, if we follow sound principles, plan realistically, execute properly and evaluate honestly. This book is a MUST READ for all managers whether in big companies or small and should be kept as a "pocket guide" reference on everyone's desk.

-Kent Harrell, Small Business Owner

Preface

You might ask what led me to title a book Stop the Monkey Business, Eight WTFs That Can Make or Break You as a Leader and Manager. Well, number one, I like monkeys. Number two, I like clever internet acronyms like WTF. I am sure you all know that WTF means "Win The Future" and I like the positiveness of that.

Nooooo! That's not really true. I do like monkeys. But I have been managing humans, and businesses, for forty years now. And there are some basic truisms that I don't understand why other people don't get.

It's like, are you kidding me? Do you really believe you are a strong manager without setting clear expectations? Guess what? Not everyone is capable of reading your mind, no matter how wonderful it might be.

Do you truly believe, in your heart of hearts, that you can be a part-time devotee of being centered on your customers and experience success? Customers now are not like the ones we had in the seventies and eighties, when they often bought from us because they had no choice. *Au contraire!* They now have many choices they can access within several minutes of being on the internet.

You are investing your time, sweat, and hard-earned money, and you really believe you can organize your business like a kids' Kool-Aid stand and create a long-term future and retirement for you and your family? Yes, I know you were hell on wheels during the first years of establishing your business. But, sorry sweetheart, you aren't good enough to keep it going without the help and contribution of others.

Finally, I know it would be a hell of a lot easier if you could manage a business in the style you are most comfortable with. However, to be a great leader you have to learn to adapt your leadership style to fit the employees and situations you are facing.

And by the way, Mr. and Mrs. Business-Owner, if you won't face the brutal facts that your business and employees are facing no one else will.

I have seen it over and over, and as Howard Beale said in the movie *Network*: "I am mad as hell, and I am not going to take it anymore!" Okay, probably not that mad. But I am tired of the bullshit, and I would like to help business owners and managers become more successful by just following a few basic tenets. To me, these are not opinions but proven strategies to be a more effective leader and manager.

Hence, it makes me feel very Shakespearean: Out Damn Monkey Business! I have some very cool WTFs that can make you a much better leader.

Enjoy.

Intro to
WTF Management

I have spent many years in business management: twelve as Senior Staff Manager, thirty as President, and most recently, seven as a Business Management Consultant. One thing has become very clear to me: despite how simple the principles of management can be, they are bloody hard to execute. It ain't easy being in charge.

Making decisions looks simple. Until the people involved are friends, or even worse, family. Then tough decision-making takes on a new meaning for even the cruelest personality. When shit is happening everywhere in your business and your life savings are hitting a new low, it is not easy to prioritize. Yeah, I get it, we need to make the customer number one. But they sure can be assholes sometimes.

Sure, I know I need a sound and sensible organizational structure. But hell, most days I'm happy if the teams just accept that they report to me.

What the F_____?! Is there an answer to this never-ending litany of problems we face when running a business?

THE WTF PRESCRIPTION:

Take two aspirins and call me in the morning. NOOOOO!! Try these first, and then take two aspirins. And don't call me.

FACE THE BRUTAL FACTS.

Quit being a wiener dog. Do what needs to be done with the people in your organization.

EXECUTE, EXECUTE, EXECUTE!

If you are so incapable that you can't set an annual plan, set at least eight to ten actions to achieve in the next quarter, and then measure them weekly.

MAKE SMART OBJECTIVES.

Objectives that are not SMART are worthless and just irritate your employees. And the rest of the universe. Either make them SMART or quit talking about it, NOW!!!

BE CUSTOMER CENTERED.

You are either customer centered, or you are not. Quit being a half-focused-on-the-customer hypocrite.

Commit, or get out of the way.

QUIT RUNNING YOUR ORGANIZATION LIKE ITS A KOOL-AID STAND.

There are proven organization standards. Not following them can be a recipe for disaster.

CORE VALUES THAT REALLY MEAN SOMETHING TO YOUR CUSTOMERS.

Core values that look like the Boy Scout Oath are bullshit!! Make it about who you are, and what makes you and your company different, or DON'T BOTHER!

LET THE TRUTH SET YOU FREE... AND QUIT IGNORING IT!

I am saying this twice. Face the brutal facts about your employees, your misguided investments, and the family members who need to go find someone else to irritate!!

LEADERSHIP: IS THERE REALLY ONE RIGHT STYLE?

No! There are four basic styles. And guess what?

You are likely only naturally good at one of them.

Ok, do I have your attention?

Now, let's take it from the top and learn some lessons that are easy to understand, but much harder to implement.

WTF #1

Facing the Brutal Facts

PREMISE

Leadership is about vision. However, it's equally about creating a climate where the truth is heard, and the brutal facts are confirmed. What the hell does that mean?

Very simply, it is one of those cultural things. If you are the type of leader who thinks that sharing how you feel is a sign of weakness, then you might have a problem with this one. You already know who I am talking about, and whether or not this is you.

Are you competitive? Do you live for personal recognition? Do you value being the best almost as much as you value money? Oops, I think I know who this guy is.

These are wonderful traits that drive us to incredible achievements.

They also are personal blindfolds – goggles that keep us from seeing the truth.

Lencioni's *The Five Dysfunctions of a Team* is the seminal writing about team building in our lifetime. He tells us the foundation of all team building is trust. Trust starts and ends with the leader. But guess what? That does not mean doing rope courses with your team. It is about being vulnerable with them daily. And vulnerability is not falling backward into their arms at a team-building event, dramatic as this all might seem. Vulnerability is about sharing your concerns, your worries, and yes, your personal failings when they occur.

Wait a minute, this can't be right. When I worked at Hilti in the eighties and nineties it was about survival of the fittest. Vulnerability, are you kidding me? That is for losers. Vulnerability is about showing your weaknesses and – *ugh* – even your feelings. And we didn't really do a lot of that in the old days of leadership.

While at Hilti I received a performance review saying I excelled in sales and profit numbers. However, I needed to stop being too emotional with my clients and employees in regard to how I felt about what we were, or were not, achieving. I asked my boss what the hell that meant, and he awkwardly replied, "Dave, you know, you kind of wear your feelings on your shirt sleeves." I struggled with that for some time. First of all, he hurt my feelings by saying that.

Oops, I know that's not very manly… ha-ha! But hey, F____ it! That's just who I am. Get over it.

At the time, I don't think I even realized this was a strength. In fact, my bosses told me it was a weakness. Looking back, I can see that one of my greatest strengths was developing strong senior teams. I shared my vulnerabilities, and my employees really liked that about me.

I saw that firsthand when one of the high-potential senior managers in Europe saw what I was doing and wanted to take a demotion to join my Latin American merry bunch of pirates. That, of course, did not play well with HQ. It was my first exposure to one of the many facets of facing the brutal facts. Really good people gravitate to leaders they trust, ones who will show them vulnerability. Especially if they are going to move their family halfway around the world to join a team.

As a leader, if you do not show vulnerability to your team, they are not going to share the brutal facts with you.

Or want to be a part of your team at all.

WTF

You know what? I get it. I was raised in the fifties. Big boys don't cry. Just rub some dirt on it and you'll be fine. Don't ever show weakness to anybody.

That's fine if we are dealing with wolves about to attack. But I am talking about your team, the guys and gals who have your back. They don't want to hear some happy horseshit about how everything is ok when it is not. Being vulnerable with your inner senior team is critical to creating an effective team overall. Listen to me very carefully. If you want them to share the brutal facts about your organization with you, including your decisions, and where your business is really going, then you must be vulnerable with them.

WTF TAKE AWAY

I had a General Manager in my early days at Hilti Latin America who was the antithesis of this concept. He was all bravado, posturing like he always had the answers. He was also the last to know when his organization screwed up. He was the last to know that he had an employee turnover problem. And the last to know that he couldn't grow his business without those so-called "little people" who did the key things that brought his company success.

His people knew. Sometimes, after a couple of pops at a local bar, they would tell me the real situation of our business in this country. He was not a bad guy, or manager. Well, he kind of was. But that is irrelevant. He just didn't get that you need the **brutal facts** to effectively manage your business.

You don't get them by asking, or by demanding. Oh no, you get them by showing vulnerability to your senior team. Don't ever forget this. Especially when you have been spending too much time reading your own press clippings. You did not get to the top of the heap on the backs of the folks who carry the mail for you. And you won't stay there if you don't establish trust with the very same people that got you there.

And as we know, trust is about vulnerability.

WTF #1 CHAPTER EXERCISE

Now let's quit talking about it and DO something to make a difference.

Become a better leader by facing and hearing the brutal facts of my employees.

Suggestions:

A. Quit being a "weenie" and own up publicly to my mistakes.
B. Share with my team members that I am sometimes clueless about where we are going.
C. Stop leading meetings with my own mouth flapping and start asking team members what they think.
D. Put 'regularly spend time with employees' on my calendar, just to get to know them.

My own actions for my SMART Objective:

Date Resp: _____

A. _____

_____

_____

B. _____

_____

_____

C. _____

_____

_____

D. _____

_____

_____

WTF #2

Execution Eats
Strategy for Breakfast

PREMISE

Jaime Dimon, CEO of JP Morgan Chase, may have said it best: "I'd rather have a first-rate execution and second-rate strategy any time than a brilliant idea and mediocre management." Supporting this further in the best-selling book *Execution: The Discipline of Getting Things Done* (co-authored with Ram Charan), former AlliedSignal CEO Larry Bossidy affirms, "Strategies most often fail because they aren't well executed."

These ideas were further developed in Gino Wickman's book *Traction, Get A Grip On Your Business*, as he talked about the idea of short-term tactical planning processes that assure weekly and quarterly execution of strategies.

Finally, Daniel Prosser confirmed it all in his book *Thirteeners*, where his research showed that only about 13% of the actions developed in long-term strategic plans ever get implemented.

This concept was counter to some of the things I learned in my early experiences, both with Gulf Oil Corporation (yes, I am older than dirt) and Hilti, the Swiss-owned company where I worked in senior management positions for over twenty-one years.

The Swiss loved to plan. Especially long-term strategic plans. It was not uncommon to create binders of detailed long-term strategies for every product line and process. It was well done, with a lot of thought. However, most of those binders went into a bookcase behind a product manager's desk, never to be seen again. Or, until the next strategic plan was developed.

Yes, they were probably incorporated into some annual planning objectives. But in most cases, the objectives were not *SMART* (Specific, Measured, Actionable, Relevant, and Timely). And as the manager got further into each year, facing changing environments and new, more important issues, they were soon forgotten.

However, the Hilti salesforce in the United States operated much differently. First, they had a process that defined what the sales rep's job should be. They also had clear-cut, long-term strategies and annual objectives. Their main difference-maker was that they managed the salesforce through written quarterly action plans that they updated every quarter, and looked at every week in their sales meeting, along with the critical sales process metrics.

Hilti was and still is recognized as one of the best direct selling forces in the U.S. When I worked there, I would often have small business owners call me and ask if I could employ their sons and daughters in a Hilti sales job for a few years. Their plan was to take them back into their own business once we had them fully trained. Their businesses were not even in similar industries, but they recognized one thing: Hilti salespeople knew how to execute a sales process. By the way, when I did employ their son or daughter my end goal was to keep them with Hilti, and they often stayed.

The key word on the success of the Hilti salesforce is *execution*. They had a well-defined process, and they knew how to manage it, from strategy down to their weekly meetings. That salesforce was successful through leadership changes, marketing changes, and even economic changes. All because they knew how to execute. And I'm not talking about killing people.

Wickman's idea of developing critical execution processes was right on target. It assured that the management team looked at and measured their progress in achieving annual objectives weekly. What successfully worked with the Hilti salesforce for over forty years also works well in managing all positions of your company.

The beauty is that strategy execution processes can be learned in an organization. The only missing component is having the discipline to stick to them with religious fervor.

So, when I say "execution eats strategy for breakfast" I am a believer. I have seen and been fortunate enough to participate in many successful instances where this has turned a business around and helped a management team start adding value to their firm.

Don't get me wrong, I am not dismissing the idea of knowing the core mission of your business or developing an idea of where the business should be in three to five years. I am just advocating the need for the real details to be in the annual plan and, even more so, in the execution tools you use to achieve it.

WTF

You know, I had thirty years of experience running businesses, sometimes successfully, and I was clueless about this one. I diligently completed three to five-year plans annually but didn't really get much from them.

I am sure many of you reading this have often participated in the full day, long-term strategy workshops where we developed missions and visions and sugar plum fairy detailed strategies. And then went for a nice dinner and a couple of pops and did not address it again. Until we repeated the same process the next year.

I probably should have refunded the consulting fees I earned doing programs that were totally focused on strategy and ignored or paid lip service to the weekly and quarterly execution of those strategies. I know we would try to tie them to the one-year plan with objectives. But, very often they weren't SMART.

Even though I had learned an excellent strategy execution process while working with a first-class salesforce during my tenure at Hilti, I had not transferred that knowledge to managing the other pieces of my businesses.

Ask the people who worked for you in the organizations where you did these detailed long-term strategies. They will tell you that they knew these were nothing more than flavor-of-the-month themes that you would soon lose sight of once you became dis-tracted by other issues.

I have a thought. **STOP DOING IT!** Who do you think Prosser surveyed in his book *Thirteeners*? Companies from Mars?

WTF TAKE AWAY

Most of us, management and employees alike, have the attention span of a well-behaved Labrador Retriever. When it comes to missions and strategies, keep it simple stupid. Focus your attention to detail on your one-year plan, and the quarterly and weekly execution processes necessary to achieve them. Most importantly, put in some planning execution processes like Hilti does for its salesforce.

All of you have weekly meetings, right? I believe they are called staff meetings, and most of them are as worthless as the proverbial tits on a boar hog.

I know how it usually goes. A lot of the companies I ran or worked for had the weekly meeting as a communication process and not for problem-solving. We would hold a weekly meeting with my senior team every week, religiously, going around the table and updating each other. HR would tell us that somebody had resigned last week, and we had to find a replacement. Finance would let us know that there was a change in payroll procedures that required a lot more work. About this time, Sales, who were on their phones texting under the table, would set their first customer meeting of the week. And then Production would bring up something totally unrelated to the discussion like, "Did you see what those crazy politicians just did on Sunday?" And then, like a pack of Labrador Retrievers, we would all go "squirrel" and bark for the next two hours about something totally unrelated to the success of our business. Have you ever seen this? (If you say no, then you are lying and need counseling.)

How do you get out of this cruel and debilitating waste of time?

Start running your weekly meetings as we did with our sales forces at Hilti. Use them to drive your critical actions that are reset and updated every quarter. Keep an eye on your most important process metrics. For sales, it was calls per day, new accounts, and new product sales. And then certainly, if there is time, address the important issue of the week.

In a nutshell, when you and your senior team get together every week, you have a strict agenda where you only talk about: your process metrics, your most important actions for the next quarter from your Plan SMART Objectives, and any other issues that need a decision now. But that's it. You do not discuss problems that don't have a ready solution or issues that should be analyzed by a smaller group and brought back to the team for decision. And the meeting is over in one to two hours. Most of the senior management teams who use this process start to see the overall time involved in their weekly meetings begin to drop very quickly.

First, they stop—and almost forbid—the chasing of squirrels during the meeting. Just as an aside, I know that squirrel chasing is a lot of fun and can produce some good ideas for strategy. Just don't do it at *this* meeting. Many of my clients find that a monthly meeting with their senior team that involves lunch or alcohol (or both) and of course some unbridled squirrel chasing is a good answer to making this work.

Second, the more they do it the better they get at it. Third, they get things accomplished in the meeting. John Kenneth Galbraith probably said it best:

"Meetings are indispensable when you don't want to do anything."

Back in the old days when I was running Hilti Latin America, I attended a standard problem-solving seminar and got enamored with action planning as a tool. So much so that I put out an edict to my colleagues on the Hilti Western Hemisphere team: My employees would no longer attend meetings of the group that did not end with a written action plan. A well-intentioned idea, but rather difficult to implement – and seen by some of my colleagues on the board as somewhat obstructionist. While you can't require it at other department heads' meetings, you can surely make it a feature of your own weekly staff meetings. Anything decided there is documented in writing to ensure it really happens. It includes what needs to be done, by whom, and a date. And we live by it with pigheaded discipline. By the way, *pigheaded* is defined by the dictionary as "willfully or perversely unyielding: <u>OBSTINATE</u>". That's a high standard, and it needs to be honored.

Oh, my goodness! We have single-handedly dealt with the biggest weakness of meetings. We talk about a lot... but NOTHING EVER GETS DONE!

That's it. If you do it with pigheaded discipline it will change you, your company, and your employees' lives.

WTF #2 CHAPTER EXERCISE

Now let's quit talking about it and DO something to make a difference.

Become a better leader by making Plan execution a weekly and quarterly event.

Suggestions:

A. Quit just staring at a monthly company dashboard and begin measuring the critical processes weekly.
B. Turn your annual plan into quarterly actions that even you and your dog can remember.
C. Reset those actions every quarter whether you need to or not.
D. Make your weekly meetings about metrics and quarterly actions (not squirrel chasing).

My own actions for my SMART Objective:

Date Resp: _____

A. _____

_____

_____

B. _____

_____

_____

C. _____

_____

_____

D. _____

_____

_____

WTF #3

If it ain't SMART you're just camping out

PREMISE

You know if every manager at the very least possessed the tool of how to make objectives SMART they would get things done, even if at times the wrong things.

In 1981, George Doran came up with the concept of SMART Objectives. He really didn't get the credit he should have for such a major development in management thought. Both Drucker and Blanchard have used the idea significantly in their own writings.

He of course took it from the idea of action plans as a way to get things done, which was the premise of many problem-solving trainings of the late seventies and early eighties. Just another simple idea: If you want to get something done, develop a sequential action plan, say who's responsible for what, and assign a due date. If it's complicated put it on a Gantt Chart.

Going back to a previous example: Even though I did realize that meetings with my senior management team at Hilti needed written action plans, I wasn't sharp enough to figure out that was also the problem with *plan objectives*. They were not action plans, nor SMART, and therefore very little ever happened.

Doran got it, though. He took the idea of action planning and crystallized it as a critical management planning tool.

Despite this concept of SMART Objectives (or, *Goals*) being touted by people like Drucker, Blanchard, and in more modern times, Wickman, they are the most underutilized good idea in the management practice of planning.

During every workshop that I have done in the last ten years almost every hand goes up when I bring up the idea of SMART Objectives and ask the participants to show me who understands and uses them. Then when I ask for an example, I get blank stares. Or worse, a half-ass answer that doesn't include the critical components.

Very simply they are nothing more than a simple acronym:

Specific
Measurable
Attainable (I prefer *Actionable,* and by whom)

Relevant
Timely

You may be asking why this is so hard to do. It's very simple really. It is hard work. And not nearly as much fun as strategic planning. Everybody likes talking about the big ideas for the business, but nobody wants to do the detailed work that will get them there. Oh yeah, everybody likes to rattle on about the new product line they need, or expansion into Latin America, and all those other things that would be cool to do in the future. But when it comes down to actually committing in writing to get it done, next week or quarter, the enthusiasm starts to die.

As I arrive at this part in the planning workshops I conduct for my clients, I have to get just a little bit ugly and push them to stay focused and do this important work.

Okay, I hear you, Dave. But what should I do to ensure my organization gets this right? Let me share one thing that I have learned as a consultant over the last seven to eight years. The biggest problem, *bar none*. I said bar none, and I mean it.

Bosses and employees are not in sync with their expectations around performance or in achieving their goals.

Yes, they think they are. The boss can tell you all the times they spoke about what needed to be done. The employee can also tell you about those previous discussions but, strangely enough, with a different memory of the conversation. How could that happen?

Number one, when they discussed what needed to be done, they kept it very general. Number two, they did not discuss what success might look like. They left it to chance that they both had the same opinion of what success would be. And finally, they never put it in writing. That's just too difficult. And Lord knows we don't have the time.

Let's change that whole bad news paradigm today. Set objectives. Make them SMART. Set them for the important things that need to be done in every area you are responsible for. And above all, **always set them in writing**.

If you can't do it SMART, or you just don't have the time, then just stop doing it altogether. It's a worthless activity that just irritates your employees.

On the other hand, if you really are committed to planning and willing to use the SMART process, get ready for the big productivity boost it will provide.

WTF #3 CHAPTER EXERCISE

Now let's quit talking about it and DO something to make a difference.

Become a better leader by making SMART Objectives a habit.

Suggestions:

A. Practice makes perfect. Learn how to write **SMART** Objectives.

B. No more annual plans with only metrics. Add 8 to 10 **SMART** Objectives and review quarterly.

C. Start using your performance appraisals and give every employee a development/improvement **SMART** Objective.

D. Don't leave another meeting just feeling good. Leave it with a SMART Objective.

My own actions for my SMART Objective:

Date Resp: _____

A. _____

_____

_____

B. _____

_____

_____

C. _____

_____

_____

D. _____

_____

_____

WTF #4

No one has the authority to disappoint a customer

PREMISE

There was a sales program back in the nineties that was all about how to manage your customers' expectations. The basic theme of this program was that sometimes customers are not very bright when it comes to assessing their own needs and don't really know what they want. So you, as the sales rep and smarter person, need to help them realize what their actual needs are.

It caught some traction for a short time, as we do sometimes have to help a customer understand their needs. But, as we now know better, the fundamental idea behind it proved wrong. Especially since the internet entered the picture. If you don't want to give them what they want, they will just find someone else who will!!

The real problem with this one is that people in production really love the idea of telling customers what they need. And why not? It makes their job easier. Also, most production teams are convinced that salespeople are not able to say no when they should. In actual fact, most customers don't really have these extravagant needs. It's primarily due to salespeople who are trying to make a buck on the backs of the manufacturing team.

You have never heard that, have you? Right! Then you have never been on the floor of a manufacturing plant that is working on a Christmas weekend to make sure the customer gets what they need when they need it.

There is a problem with this thinking. It's that almost all modern companies today say they are customer driven. Unfortunately, wishing to be customer driven doesn't make it so. You can't be customer driven only when it fits the production schedule. It is just as critical on holiday weekends as it is on any other ordinary weekend. Customer driven is one of those things in life where you either are or you are not.

Being 50%, 75%, or even 95% customer driven doesn't work. Customers expect you to be customer driven every time you serve them, or they will simply go online and find someone else.

Do you know the numbers on losing customers? According to an Oracle study, 89% of customers begin doing business with a competitor following a poor customer service experience.

It is six times more expensive to acquire a new customer than it is to keep a current one. Couple that with the truism that news of bad customer service reaches over twice as many people as praise for a good customer experience, and I think you have an open and shut case for being 100% customer service driven.

Hey, I am an old production guy at heart, and I know most salespeople are selfish and overpaid. But get over it! It is not about the salesman. Lean over amigo, let me whisper something in your ear: **It is about the customer!!!**

WTF TAKEAWAY

I am not just making this shit up. I ran a printing company for several years in my career as a "hired gun" president.

They were into being customer driven, but not always at 100%. Early in my reign as their leader, I came upon a 3-million-piece decal order and found the shipping supervisor placing handfuls of decals into already stacked and ready-to-package decals. I was new to printing so I asked what he was doing. He replied matter-of-factly that they were "seeding" culls into the packages of good decals. It was only 100,000 of the 3 million, so who would know? It also improved the scrap percentage that they were being graded on by their plant manager.

This print job was for a charity that sent these out in mailers all over the country to raise money for their cause. All I could think of was if just one got into the hands of a senior manager of either the charity or the mail house who was handling the project it would ruin the reputation the ownership had been working years to build.

I called a meeting the next day and gave my (slightly) famous speech. "No one has the authority to disappoint a customer but myself or the owner. Anyone who doesn't get that can find somewhere else to work." Trust me, they heard me when I said that. Nobody cried – but I hoped we were close to that type of reaction.

The very next day we started to push the core value of being customer driven.

We put in an employee recognition program that would find one or two people every week who went the extra mile to service a customer, and gave them a Walmart card, a good dose of thank-yous, and public praise.

It had such an impact on the employees being more customer driven that I had several key accounts comment on how attentive we had become to our customers and how much they appreciated it.

I had to prove it about a year later when there was a slight color miss on another one of those large orders. My sales rep reminded me of my earlier speech on the subject of never disappointing a customer. The owner of the business measured me on the profitability of the firm, and I knew that an $80,000 loss in one month due to a product that was well printed, if just a little off in the color spectrum, was not going to be an easy explanation. But I also knew just how much positive revenue our customer driven culture was producing. I replaced the order with the right color.

When I met with that customer several years later their president said, "Doing the right thing and rescuing that order was one of the primary reasons we used your company. You stand behind your work." I bet they are still customers of that print shop today.

So, what do I do to make sure that "the customer is number one" is not just lip service that eventually bites me in the ass? It starts with this simple premise: If the customer is number one then we *all* must love our customers. And that, of course, starts with your *Core Values* (*see Chapter VI*).

But there's even more to being customer driven than just the talk. Who are the people you hire for your key positions? If you hire a controller who thinks that their number one responsibility is to always save money, even at the expense of your customers and the people who service them, then you don't really get it.

WTF #4 CHAPTER EXERCISE

Now let's quit talking about it and DO something to make a difference.

Become a better leader by making my business customer centered.

Suggestions:

A. Start enforcing "No one has the authority to disappoint a customer."
B. Start recognizing and loving your employees who make the customers smile.
C. Employees who cannot love your customers need to go torment someone else's customers.
D. Scare your Finance Manager and give every employee the authority to solve a customer's problem.

My own actions for my SMART Objective:

Date Resp: _____

A. _____

_____

_____

B. _____

_____

_____

C. _____

_____

_____

D. _____

_____

_____

WTF #5

Poor Organization can cost you a lot of money

PREMISE

I recently did a strategy workshop with a fast-growing business that is partially owned by a venture capitalist. When we started to look at the hired-gun president's organization, I saw that he had five outside sales reps who all reported directly to him, three different foremen who were running his production facility, his engineering manager (on top of the engineering work he himself was doing), *and* the assistant/accounting-manager (who also ran HR and occasionally functioned as office manager).

What is wrong with this picture?

How about, twelve direct reports from multiple functional areas that required close coordination, as several people were responsible for some of the same areas.

I raised the issue of *span of control* in our workshop, and the president was not amused. His people were though, as they already knew this. They just wondered how long I would be able to pursue this point before being shut down. Not long! He quickly informed me that he worked for venture capitalists, and they had certain expectations on cost. And it all started with people. So, for now, he couldn't afford a plant manager or director of sales. That was my last workshop with that group. I often wonder what we could have achieved if I could have gotten the point of span of control across to that boss.

I understand the importance of lean organizations. I too worked for a venture capital company earlier in my career. But I also learned, when growing Hilti's Latin America division at a 25% clip for over ten years, that real growth and profitability do not come by just cutting costs.

When it comes to organization you have to spend some money to build a business that can sustain its success. Let me repeat that a little differently with an old adage: **You have to spend money to make money!**

I remember one of my first annual plan presentations to my venture capitalist boss. I got the traditional lecture about saving money when I proposed establishing a nationwide key-account sales organization to really boost the growth of this small business they had just purchased.

I was not used to being micromanaged by the board and popped off, "If you f___ing know so much about direct selling, why did you hire me to run this company?" I thought I would most likely be looking for a new position. However, at dinner he let me know that he liked that I fought for my ideas, and we went on to achieve and exceed our growth plans for this business. We also added ALL of the key-account managers that I had requested. I had already learned at Hilti that you can't cut your way to business success by *not* having the people you need. It helped me continue a successful career in growing businesses.

Louis Allen had an excellent section in their management development program on the "Principles of Organization" that I had utilized in training Hilti International executives in the eighties and nineties. I still use it today.

Principle of Specialization

According to this principle, the entire work of an enterprise must be shared among the subordinates based on their qualifications, abilities, and skills. Hence, effective organization can be achieved through the specialization of shared work. I have used this with my clients to justify the centralization of all customer service activities, especially when they are in different departments and locations. I cannot think of a time once customer service was centralized that customer offerings were not markedly improved, and savings not significantly increased.

Principle of Functional Definition

This principle states that all the work in an enterprise must be fully and clearly described to both the managers and subordinates. For instance, each of the following must be clearly described to all of the people working in a department: the initial work that must be done and the related metrics to measure it; the authority of the managers and responsibility of the workers; and how they all relate to each other. Hence, clarification of authority and responsibility helps in the growth of an organization. I have coached bosses and subordinates for over forty years now, and the number one problem I have discovered when brought in to solve a conflict is unclear expectations of what the position is. I know job descriptions are boring, but they do serve a purpose. Until clear expectations of what a job entails are done *in writing*, they are not really clear.

Let's stop right here. Do you hear me?! Develop written job descriptions for your critical employees. It makes a difference!!

Also, if you like to use incentives to reward your senior team, neglecting to set up clear and separate functional definitions can make it almost impossible to motivate success with bonuses. There's nothing more demotivating than giving a bonus that I cannot totally influence the results of because of ill-defined sharing of accountability.

Principles of Supervision, or Span of Control

This principle speaks to the span of control, which shows the number of employees that a single manager can control and handle efficiently. The question is this: Is there a magic number for the span of control to effectively manage people?

No magic number exists, as it is impacted by the location of the people, the complexities of their work, and the need for the boss's frequent presence. At Hilti, we discussed this often as we grew the sales organization and arrived at the number of eight to ten sales reps for one area sales manager. However, for someone managing multiple work functions and locations, eight to ten could prove to be too much to manage effectively.

I learned this one first-hand when I managed Hilti's Latin American division. I had presidents in eight different countries, and another five direct reports who ran the business on a functional basis. If you took a look at me in my last years as president of this organization, I was very close to a mess. Every Friday my assistant gave me a plane ticket, cash, and my speech–written in Spanish–for when I arrived. I was, in a word, "tapped out" in my ability to manage my direct reports. I had a big span of control problem and it was near impossible to do what I needed to do to continue to help that organization grow.

Principle of Unity of Command

According to this principle, one subordinate is accountable to only one superior at a time. This helps in preventing a lack of communication and feedback and ensures a quick response.

This is a tough one in smaller organizations when there is no choice but to share certain resources. But at the very least, the principle of organization can help when you realize the ineffectiveness created by subordinates who start shopping bosses to find the one who will give them the answer they need.

I remember working with the senior team of a very successful tech company and discussing their organization, which had an owner who was sharing the management of several functions with his hired-gun president. I asked the senior team if this was ever a problem and they all shook their heads no, like a pack of bobblehead dolls. I called bullshit and then asked, "So you guys never go to one or the other of your two bosses because you think you will get the answer you want?" There was dead silence as everyone waited to see if one of the bosses would deal with my insolence. Fortunately, their marketing vice president spoke up – this was not her first rodeo – and confirmed that of course they shopped their bosses based on who would give a favorable response. She went on to say that it was also sometimes a problem for their employees lower in the organization. We went on to have a healthy discussion and both the owner and president took actions to clarify their organization responsibility.

WTF

So, to all of you "bean-counter" presidents who think you really make companies grow by being Attila the Hun on expenses, it ain't true and the best of you already know it. I understand a culture of lean organization is important to profitability. But that attitude cannot trump (and I don't mean our former President) following proper organization principles.

My former client, who was convinced he would keep his venture capitalist boss happy by not spending money on necessary people, will eventually pay for this in costly lost opportunities.

If you are currently having problems with some of your subordinates getting the work done when and how you want it, do a little self-analysis. Have you been clear, in writing, about what you want done? Try it, you might be surprised by the change in results.

Also, look at those situations where you have people trying to navigate pleasing two or more bosses. It always creates some problems. If you can't afford to change it now then at least recognize the issues and improve the joint communication of the multiple bosses involved.

WTF TAKEAWAY

Doing organization development like you are running a Kool-Aid stand is a recipe for disaster. Regularly look at the way you are organized and make sure you are following the basic principles of organization. Also, identify the organization you need for your future growth plans and make the changes necessary to achieve them, rather than expecting your people to just work harder.

Do some self-introspection on how you impact your organization's integrity. Do you regularly hold employees accountable for loosely defined expectations? Are you asking your best and brightest people to take on impossible spans of control simply to save a few bucks? When you do this, you end up losing the best people. The mediocre ones unfortunately stay with you.

Last, are you creating a situation of "two bosses" for your employees by going around your senior managers and dealing with them directly and causing chaos and confusion for them – and pissing off your senior team in one fell swoop?

WTF #5 CHAPTER EXERCISE

Now let's quit talking about it and DO something to make a difference.

Become a better leader by developing an organization built for success.

Suggestions:

A. Look at your people organization annually. Admit and adjust the compromises done for friends and family.
B. Stop doing things because that is how it's always been done.
C. Keep an eye on span of control, and don't abuse your best people.
D. Don't create organization confusion by walking around like "Charles In-Charge". Honor the reporting lines of your team.

My own actions for my SMART Objective:

Date Resp: _____

A. _____

_____

_____

B. _____

_____

_____

C. _____

_____

_____

D. _____

_____

_____

WTF #6

Core Values: If You Don't Mean It... Don't Bother

PREMISE

Core values became popular in the late nineties and early aughts. For most companies, they were done more for show – prettied up by the marketing department, framed and placed at the business entry.

Those core values were fairly innocuous. Unless you were visibly not aligned with them, in which case you'd be better off not having them at all. Core values are one of the most misunderstood tools of the management profession.

First off, it *is* okay to have a few core values that come from the Boy Scout Oath, but that's not really what it's all about. Lencioni called them "permission to play" values. I mean, do you really think your competition doesn't care if they have dishonest people or folks that have no integrity? Give me a break! Trust me, they care.

When we have a permission-to-play core value like honesty, do we really mean it under *all* circumstances? If someone comes to work dressed in less than impressive business attire, or with a new haircut that's not so hot, do we put our honesty core value into practice and tell them they don't look very good? Or does that value only apply to certain circumstances?

As Lencioni pointed out, many companies have core values that are chosen to help them change behavior in order to solve problems they currently have.

I get it. Of course, you want to have people who can fit the culture you need to grow your business for the future. The problem with that is that a company can only handle the culture change of maybe one core value they don't currently practice or represent. Core values are a tough business, and just creating one you don't already possess is very difficult.

The rest of the core values should reflect your strengths as a team, and you simply build on them to be even more successful. I hope you have heard me here. This is another example of wishin' don't make it so. Core values, in most cases, should reflect why people even buy from you in the first place.

Where I have had the most success in using these core values to change a company's culture has been in focusing on the strengths that make them unique to their customers. If customer centered is one of the distinctive abilities that help your company to retain customers, then maybe empathy is a good core value to look for and nurture in your employees. If getting a product done 100% correctly the first time is a key driver of gaining new accounts, perhaps attention to detail should be a core value.

Of course, the key to this whole thing isn't just identifying the core values in your organization. It is also living them and putting them into practice in the human resources processes of your company.

Do you look for the core values in prospective employees when you interview them? The way you go about that is not by directly asking them if they have, say, empathy for customers. Although, I have seen it happen in job interviews where the employer will actually ask the question, "How are you on empathy for customers?" The applicant answers, "I am great at that," and the manager nods their head and moves on to the next question. No!!! That is not how you do it.

A real simple point here on interviewing people for a job: Past behavior is the best predictor of future behavior. So, very simply, it is asking them to give you examples from their past positions where they personally went the extra mile for a customer. And FYI, if they look at you like a deer in the headlights when you ask that question, they probably don't have that core value. People who have empathy for their customers like to tell you about it.

Also, if you are going to make core values part of your company culture, they need to be included in your performance appraisal process. Employees who aren't getting it need to be told that it is required behavior. And if they need training to get there, then help them. But if they cannot eventually embrace the core values, they need to go irritate another company.

Back in my days of running Human Resources for a large company, team player – or being a good collaborator – was a core value. I had an employee that was a genius when it came to technical areas of compensation, but clueless when it came to working as a team member with the rest of my department. As good as his ideas were, they were not enough to replace the "roadkill" he would leave in his path when he led a critical project with the other members of the team. He eventually had to find another place to work. I really did cry when he left (he was a close friend). But I had to admit that it was time, as Collins says in his book *Good to Great*, "…to confront the brutal facts."

The biggest impact you can have on institutionalizing core values is recognizing people when they do it right. And it's critical you first promote the people who embrace those same core values.

The most significant impact I had as a company president on culture and core values was done by setting up frequent recognitions of people who were doing it right. When we did this, and we did it often, people would actually remember the core values and start to live them.

I wasn't always consistent in doing this, so I had to set up an activity on my calendar for every Friday at 9:00 AM. "Go find someone doing something right." It would normally start by me going by the plant manager's office and asking if he had recognized a core value in anyone this week. Often his answer was no, as he'd been too busy. I would then invite him with me into the plant, armed with Walmart gift cards, and we would find someone who had done something extraordinary for a customer, publicly thank them, and give them a gift card.

The plant had about eighty employees. We did this every week for a year, and by the end, we had done eighty recognitions of forty different people. Some never got recognized (oh so sad) and others got two or more (I loved that!). This concerted effort by our management team changed the culture and made a noticeable impact on the customer service we were providing to our clients.

The last part of institutionalizing core values is that the senior team must not only live them but also evangelize them.

WTF

Core values that your employees can't even remember are worthless.

Boy Scout Oath core values do not really move the needle as far as culture change that helps increase the value of your business.

Aspirational core values that half of your employees and executives don't understand, or lack the skill set to achieve, are not only worthless but also damaging to your credibility with both employees and customers.

Don't set core values unless you are ready for the sustained hard work of institutionalizing them.

WTF TAKEAWAY

If you want to do something with both your team and the culture that can change your company, increase its monetary value, and improve sustainability, set some core values that reflect who you are and what differentiates your company from the competition.

Then set a SMART Objective to institutionalize them through hiring practice, employee development, and a planned recognition program. And pursue all those actions with pigheaded discipline. Don't be surprised if your employees, customers, and shareholders all start to notice the positive improvements in your business.

WTF #6 CHAPTER EXERCISE

Now let's quit talking about it and DO something to make a difference.

Become a better leader by institutionalizing your company's core values.

Suggestions:

    A. There has to be some reason(s) why people buy from you. Start emphasizing those reasons.

    B. Quit asking candidates if they are good at something. Instead, ask for examples of how they have done it in the past.

    C. When employees live your company's Core Values, give them a gift (like a Walmart card) and tell them thank you.

    D. When employees *don't* live your Core Values, give them "an apple and a road map" to find someplace else to work.

My own actions for my SMART Objective:

Date Resp: _____

A. _____

    _____

    _____

B. _____

    _____

    _____

C. _____

    _____

    _____

D. _____

    _____

    _____

WTF #7

Spend more time on "Not Demotivating Employees"

PREMISE

Jim Collins imparted a lot of wisdom in his book *Good to Great*. But I think the most important was: confront the brutal facts. I have already referenced it several times in this book, and now you are going to hear it again.

His thoughts on hiring decisions and firing decisions are needed by almost every client I have worked with in my career.

Simply put, if a new recruit doesn't look or feel right then don't hire them. When it comes to an employee who's not fitting in, performing marginally at best, and is not responding to your development activities, they need to find another company to irritate.

The most common employee issue I find when coaching business owners and leaders is the long service employee who is below satisfactory in their employee rating and is just not hacking it. When we talk to them about areas to improve, they nod their heads up and down. Yet, when we check in again a month or two later, no change. Or minimal improvement, at best.

These are normally not issues like being a better engineer or accountant, but instead more routine requests like showing up on time, doing follow through with other team members, or checking their own work for obvious errors.

Some of my clients find facing the brutal facts to be too negative, so I sometimes use a phrase that is biblical in its origin. I still can hear the revival pastor at the little church in western Oklahoma that we attended with my grandma, shouting at the top of his lungs, "The Truth Will Set You Free!", right before the choir belted out "He Lives" (and I got taken to the back room for pinching my brother). I don't think he was talking about managing people when he shouted this out.

But I'll tell you what it does apply to, under-performers who can't change after repeated requests to do so. Often, they are not very happy with their position either and a change of scenery may do them good. And what about the good performers who are busting their asses to get it done? Do you think they appreciate you keeping folks who don't perform? Dealing with this truth of poor performance will set you free from all the worthless energy you spend worrying about it.

WTF

I was working with one of the top charities in Tulsa not so long ago, helping them set their strategies and core values.

As part of the discussion, we rated the senior team on the organization's core values, and then talked about how the rest of the employees were doing with them.

It appears they had a group of employees in their warehouse who were not very good at being empathetic with their clients, which was one of the organization's core values. They would make fun of the clients behind their backs and, in some cases, to their faces.

I said, "Well, then talk to them. And if they can't change then replace them with employees who *are* empathetic with your clients." I remember the Operations Director looking at me incredulously and saying, "We can't do that. These are long-service employees, and we are a charity."

I almost lost it. But, as calmly as I could, I replied, "So you care more about the motivation of your long service, poor performers than you do the hardworking SOB's who are helping you provide service to your clients. And what about the stewardship core value, where you make a promise to spend your donors' hard-earned money wisely, delivering needed services to the disadvantaged."

We had a great discussion after that outburst. And they did clean out the "bad eggs" in their organization, much to the applause of the rest of their workforce.

WTF TAKE AWAY

I learned this very early in my career when doing union negotiation with the Steel Workers in Cleveland, Ohio. The union steward I was working with was a gruff old dog, named Alfred Capone. (I know. I thought it was kind of odd too.)

I was a young, twenty-seven-year-old Director of Labor Relations on his first assignment with this division and union. I think old Al must have taken pity on me, as he started off with some advice. "Hey kid let me tell you somethin' about unions. It's not complicated, amigo. As long as you treat people the same - you college guys call it consistency - you can treat them like crap." I looked at Al like, *really*, and said, "Are you f___ing kidding me?!" He replied very nicely, "No, kid. And don't forget to get me the new fish locator for my boat." I was not involved in that, but my attorney may have been.

I was kind of offended by this remark at first. But as I thought about it over the years, Ol' Al wasn't too far off the mark. If you treat people consistently, at the very least it won't demotivate them. But if you give the poor performers special treatment by not requiring them to meet everyone else's standards, you will really pay the price. Just remember what that revival preacher said long ago, "The Truth Will Set You Free."

WTF #7 CHAPTER EXERCISE

Now let's quit talking about it and DO something to make a difference.

Become a better leader by not demotivating my employees.

Suggestions:

    A. Honestly evaluate my current team. Even the ones I like. And my brother-in-law.
    B. Sit down with the ones who need to understand brutal facts and set an improvement plan.
    C. Tell people what you want them to do rather than just "wishin' for it".

My own actions for my SMART Objective:

Date Resp: _____

A. _____

_____

_____

B. _____

_____

_____

C. _____

_____

_____

D. _____

_____

_____

WTF #8

All Leadership Styles are Right... Sometimes

This is my last WTF, and maybe the most important one. It really needs to be here because it addresses a key question in management thought: Is there one right style of management that we all need to learn to be effective managers?

PREMISE

There is a lot of discussion on whether there is one right management style or type of leader. From my experience, I not only don't think so but also believe this is the start of dangerous thinking. In my firm, we use the Trimetrix assessment to evaluate candidates for senior management positions. It takes a look at the classic DISC profile of managers, as well as their principal motivators, to help us understand who can best fit a job. One of my colleagues is convinced that there is a single profile that can describe a successful company president. Everything I know about successful CEOs says this is incorrect thinking. Just looking at Apple can tell us a lot about this way of thinking. Steve Jobs and Tim Cook are very different people with equally differing profiles. However, each fit very well in their management situations, based on having the right management style to fit their employees at that time in the development of Apple. Good management is about adapting your style to fit the needs of your team.

The epicenter of good management thought was Blanchard and Hersey's work on situational leadership. Go read it and put it to memory, now.

1. There is no right way of leading people.
2. There are four ways that fit, based on the circumstance.
   A. Telling people what to do because they don't know any better and that is what they need to hear.
   B. Selling people on what to do, because they now have enough knowledge to ask a few questions.
   C. Participating with your employees in decision-making because they are now more concerned about what you are doing. And that concern is the first step in helping you actually utilize their knowledge to increase the success of your business.
   D. Delegating to the employees who actually have the maturity and com-

mitment to deal with your business. But done so with clear expectations, often in writing, and not just abdicating your responsibilities with the hope that they have the same understanding as you do what a "good job" looks like.

3. Only 1% of the population is even capable of operating in all four styles. Learn to operate in three of the styles and you will be a manager of epic proportions.

WTF

Many years ago, during the time of dinosaurs and monkeys who talked, the leading thought was that there were two primary ideas about management. You could be either a *Theory X* style: authoritative and telling people what to do, or a *Theory Y:* participative and working in concert with your employees to decide what to do and execute. The prevailing thought at that time was that Theory Y was correct and would lead us to a time of prosperity and happiness. However, there was a big problem with that. Some of the most successful managers of all time were pure Theory X in style, and it worked. It's not just Steve Jobs who fits into this style but also Jack Welch, among others, if we're being honest. Along came Hersey and Blanchard to inform us of what was really happening.

They found out, through very simple research, that there are four basic styles. Any of which are appropriate, depending on the maturity level of the employee. Wow, then it's very simple. We just have to adjust our leadership style to fit the maturity level of our employees. Yeah right, most of us are only good at one style. Or two, at best. How in the hell can we make that work? It's simple. Start spending your management development time learning how to operate in the two or three styles you are not comfortable with.

You know what? It actually works. I know if you are a direct person who likes to tell people what to do it is hard to be participative, or even delegatory, with your employees. But when you do, especially with your most mature employees, the results are so impressive you will keep trying until you get better at it.

I had an employee at my printing company who was very successful at running our shipping and receiving with a participative style. I came out one day to see where we were at on a very large 4-million-part decal order that had to ship by the end of the week. I asked how it was going and Jack said, "It's a mess. These people have no experience in what they are doing, and HR should be fired for even bringing them in." I looked at what was going on and agreed it was a total mess. I offered Jack the idea of organizing the work of packing decals into three very simple activities: counting the decals into groups of 100, running them through the shrink wrap machine, and then packing them into boxes of 250,000. Jack kind of agreed, and I moved on to other things going on in the plant. When I returned that afternoon, he was almost enthusiastic as he informed me we were on schedule to ship the decals, and that I needed to tell HR that these were very good people she had brought in for this project. What happened in between the morning discussion and later that same afternoon? Very simply, Jack went from a participative style to a very strong and direct style of telling each person what they needed to do. Hell, they had no experience in packing three-million-part decal orders. In fact, who would? When you left them to make their own decisions regarding what to do in an area they had no real knowledge of, they performed miserably and were, in fact, quite pissed off. Have you ever heard employees say, "just tell me what you want me to do and leave me the hell alone"? Well, I have.

However, when you explicitly told them what to do, they received it well, and actually became good performers.

I often remembered this learning experience when facing other situations where otherwise good people were not performing and found it a useful reference on how to improve performance through the correct leadership style.

WTF TAKEAWAY

Back to my colleague, who thinks there is one right leadership style and behavior. He is a very bright man and a much better student of human behavior than I am. But I have no doubt that he is wrong. The right leadership style is being able to adapt to any of the four styles when called for, based on the maturity of the employee. You get this one right and you are on your way to becoming a very successful leader of your company.

Finally, I leave you with one last thought for success: HAVE A SENSE OF HUMOR.

It is not the end of the world when we don't achieve an objective. When an employee doesn't work out it just means they might be better served with another company. Take time with your team to enjoy the craziness of running a business together. The fact is that there are no totally right answers. The truism is that often it's just the luck of the draw that leads to our success.

Remember that the best part of all of this is enjoying the ride together with our team.

WTF #8 CHAPTER EXERCISE

Now let's quit talking about it and DO something to make a difference.

Become a better leader by becoming more versatile in the four leadership styles.

Suggestions:

A. In which of the four leadership styles am I a fish out of water?

B. Start using that style and ask for feedback, even if it hurts.

C. Evaluate my employees on their maturity level and start using the style that fits them, not me.

D. Ask a mentor or trusted employee to jerk my chain (privately) and let me know when I am using the wrong leadership style.

My own actions for my SMART Objective:

Date Resp: _____

A. _____

_____

_____

B. _____

_____

_____

C. _____

_____

_____

D. _____

_____

_____

Chapter 9

One Last Thought Before
We Say Adieu

Okay, I said I was done, but I would be remiss if I did not go back over the premises of the book and make sure you actually heard me.

Number One: Share your feelings and brutal facts with your employees. Team building starts with trust. Trust starts with being vulnerable with your team. Hey, you do the math! If you want a team who will the go the extra mile with you, this is the beginning of it.

Number Two: Execution Eats Strategy for Breakfast. Do you hear me? Do you get it? Doing what your customers want, every time, without failure. That is what grows your business. Yeah, I know you also have to worry about the things you need to do or change so you can grow. Yes, that takes some strategic thinking. But don't ever, ever forget what brought you here in the first place – It's EXECUTION!!

Number Three: If it ain't SMART you are just camping out. How many times do I have to say it? Dammit, if it's important *put it in writing* so that you can remember together what you agreed to. Neglecting to set clear expectations, for boss and employee, is the number one problem in employee relations.

Number Four: No one has the authority to disappoint a customer. Are you hearing me? No one. Not the Production VP, not the Controller and, God forbid, not you, Mr. or Mrs. President. This is not some cool thing we say to look like we are with it. Either become 100% customer centered or quit talking about it.

Number Five: Poor organization can cost you a lot of *dinero*. Do not go off and try to solve long-term problems like succession and business operations until you set your organization right. Otherwise, you are just wasting your time.

Number Six: Core Values. This is not just some easy, pleasy HR concept. Core values can change your corporate life. Get them right!! Live them!! And get ready for a corporate transformation.

Number Seven: Face the brutal facts and let the truth set you free. You know, there is a consulting firm in the United States who makes a lot more money than I do offering nothing more than helping their clients to face the brutal facts. They even brag about it. Like it's a badge to wear with others in the profession. I get it. Though to me it's not that simple. I want to treat people fairly and give them several chances to improve and correct their performance. But when their behavior starts to impact the motivation of my good employees then it is time for me to act. The biggest problem I face in my practice with small businesses is that they do not deal with employee problems whenever they should... or sometimes at all.

If you have an employee who cannot behave and fit the core values of your organization, they need to go torture someone else.

Finally, there is no Holy Grail of leadership style. There are four basic ones, and the quicker you figure out what they are the closer you are to becoming an effective leader. Then you just have to start working on the ones you aren't naturally good at and make them part of your management repertoire. Unfortunately, it ain't easy, and it will take time to start to feel comfortable in all four. Plus, I haven't even really clarified that they are only effective if you are also good at assessing the maturity level of your employees.

Like my mama, God rest her soul, taught me when she made me take piano lessons when I was seven years old: Practice makes perfect, David Leroy (she liked using my middle name for emphasis). She made me practice that damn piano for an hour almost every day until I was fourteen. I am a pretty good salesman and, somehow, I convinced her that no more practicing that damn piano would help me graduate with honors from high school. I lied.

But you know what, practice works. And while I am no concert pianist, I can still play a passable piano tune at seventy years old.

Start practicing your leadership styles like my mom made me do for an hour every day, and you will be surprised at your growth as a leader.

Bibliography

- Allen, Louis. Organization Principles: Principles of Professional Management. McGraw Hill, 1973.
- Blanchard, Ken. *Situational Leadership Theory.* Pfeiffer Wiley, 1998.
- Bossidy, Larry, and Ram Charan. *Execution: The Discipline of Getting Things Done.* Crown Publishing Group, 2002.
- Collins, James. Confronting the Brutal Facts: Good to Great. Harper Collins, 2001.
- Collins, James, and Jerry Porras. (1996, September-October). *Core Values: Building Your Company's Vision.* Harvard Business Review.
- Doran, George. (1981, November) There's a S.M.A.R.T. way to write management's goals and objectives. *Management Review.* 70 (11): 35-36
- Hersey, Paul and Ken Blanchard. Management of Organizational Behavior: Utilizing Human Resources. 1969. Prentice-Hall, 1996.
- Lencioni, Patrick. *Five Dysfunctions of a Team.* Jossey-Bass, 2009.
- Lencioni, Patrick. (2002, July). *Make Your Values Mean Something.* Harvard Business Review.
- Lumet, S. (Director). (1976) *Network.* [Film]. Metro-Goldwyn-Mayer

- Oracle. (2013). *Global Insights on Succeeding in the Customer Experience Era*. Oracle.com. https://www.oracle.com/us/global-cx-study-2240276.pdf

  Prosser, Daniel. *Thirteeners*. Greenleaf Book Group Press, 2015.
- Wickman, Gino. *Traction, Get A Grip on Your Business*. BenBella Books, 2012.

About the Author

 Dave Cleveland, a life-long Tulsan, pursued his first career in Human Resources, after completing his MBA at the University of Tulsa.

His early success as a 20 something Director of Personnel for two international companies led to his getting a chance to actually run a business before age 35, as President of Hilti's Latin America division. Over the next 30 years he went on to lead several other family businesses, in several different industries. He's a big believer in experience being the greatest teacher, and likes to tell his clients, "Hell, if I can just teach you half the things I have screwed up over the course of my career, you have a decent chance of being successful."

Having tried retirement over 7 years ago, where he "failed miserably", he is now the Managing Partner of Corporate Performance Group. His business focuses on working with business owners and presidents to develop strategies that can lead to achieving their personal long-term vision of success.

Dave has a strong passion for the Not-for-Profit sector and has served as Board Chair for many of them in the Tulsa and Oklahoma area. His commitment continues today, with over one third of his consulting time dedicated to helping their boards and leadership establish strong executable strategies.

Like What You've Read?

Please Leave a Review!